For wildlife warrior Debbie, and her daughters Jasmine and Jade – SOR

For Archer, my junior zoologist, who inspires me to stay curious – AH

A catalogue record for this book is available from the National Library of Australia.

ISBN: 9781486315918 (hbk)
ISBN: 9781486315925 (epdf)
ISBN: 9781486315932 (epub)

Published by:
CSIRO Publishing
Private Bag 10
Clayton South VIC 3169
Australia

Telephone: +61 3 9545 8400
Email: publishing.sales@csiro.au
Website: www.publish.csiro.au
Sign up to our email alerts: publish.csiro.au/earlyalert

Edited by Dr Kath Kovac
Cover, text design and typeset by Astred Hicks, Design Cherry
Printed in China by Leo Paper Products Ltd

Map on page 30 by okili77/Shutterstock.com and Astred Hicks, with range data supplied by Debbie Saunders.

The views expressed in this publication are those of the author and illustrator and do not necessarily represent those of, and should not be attributed to, the publisher or CSIRO.

Jun22_01

CSIRO acknowledges the Traditional Owners of the lands that we live and work on across Australia and pays its respect to Elders past and present. CSIRO recognises that Aboriginal and Torres Strait Islander peoples have made and will continue to make extraordinary contributions to all aspects of Australian life including culture, economy and science. CSIRO is committed to reconciliation and demonstrating respect for Indigenous knowledge and science. The use of Western science in this publication should not be interpreted as diminishing the knowledge of plants, animals and environment from Indigenous ecological knowledge systems.

Note for readers: Words in bold are explained in the glossary at the end of the book.

Note for teachers: Teacher notes are available at:
https://www.publish.csiro.au/book/8062/#forteachers

STEPHANIE OWEN REEDER
ASTRED HICKS

Swifty

THE SUPER-FAST PARROT

CSIRO
PUBLISHING

Deep in the **hollow** of an ancient tree,
three baby parrots snuggle up close.

Their downy **crowns** tremble as mum
feeds them sweet gum-blossom **nectar**.

Mum awakes to the sound of
sugar glider claws scrabbling on bark.

Two of her babies have gone!

Only Swifty remains.

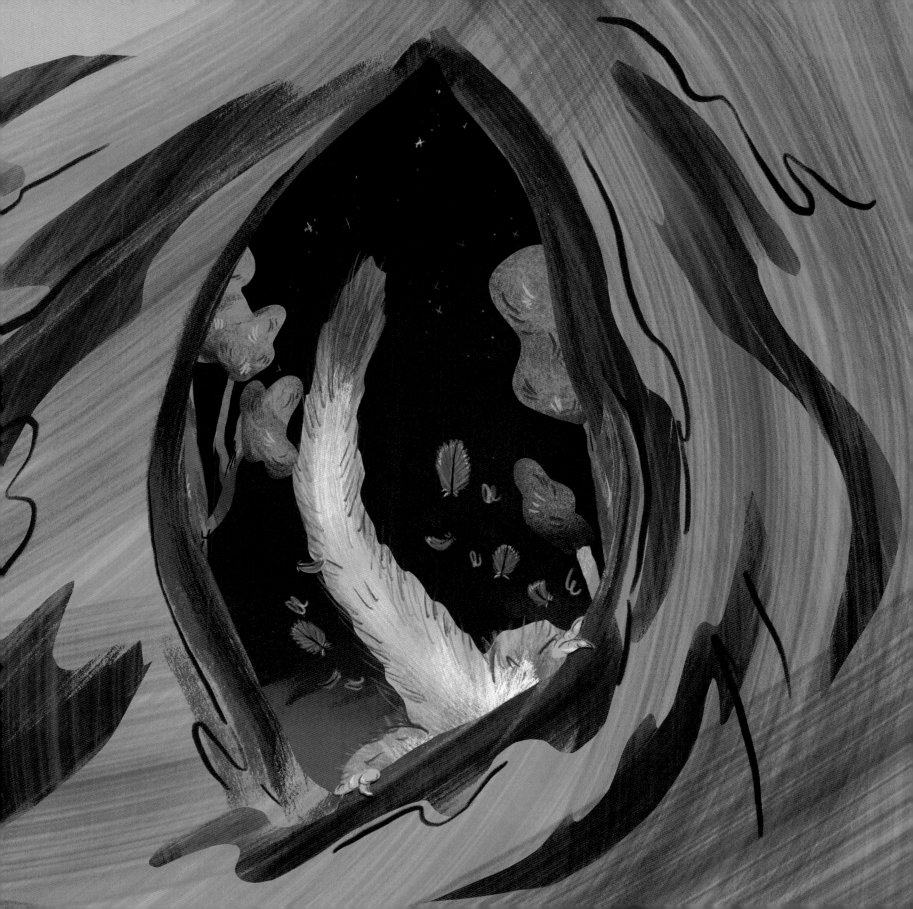

As she grows, rainbow colours flood Swifty's feathers.

She practises flying with the other **fledglings**, zipping and zooming through the trees.

When autumn arrives,
the swift parrots
frantically feast.

Swifty gobbles **lerps** from leaves and scoops sticky nectar from gum blossoms.

It's time to head north.

The parrots follow the **blossom trail**
across the wild waters of Bass Strait.

Swifty flies among them, ready for adventure.

On the mainland, blossoms are scarce,
so the parrots move on.

Swifty keeps up, but others
are not so lucky.

Swifty cavorts around a fluttering flag.

She shimmies across a sparkling harbour.

Faster and faster
she flies.

Swifty lies winded and wounded.

Then screeching birds attack!

But gentle hands save her.

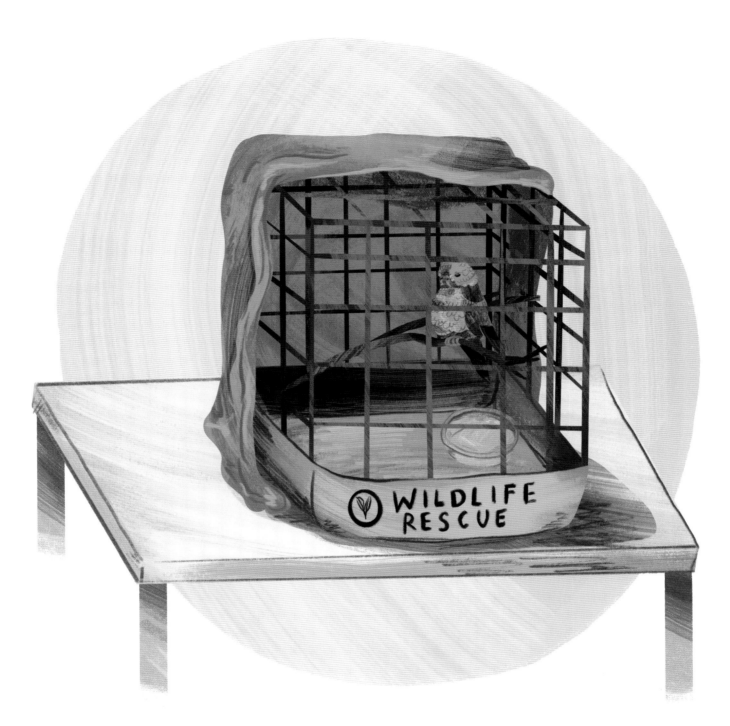

Soft voices calm her.

And days of rest revive her.

It's time to return to the wild.

A tree erupts with **chirruping**, bell-like calls.

Out shoots Swifty – straight up into the **canopy** and the company of friends.

Spring calls.
Swifty flies south,

swooping
and wheeling

over forests and plains.

Across the white-capped waters of
Bass Strait she travels, back down
to where the blue gums blossom.

But her old tree is taken.

Will she ever find a nesting hollow?

Swifty races across a rippling channel
to the safety of a small island.

She searches among
the blossoming trees.

And there she finds the
perfect place to nest.

Home at last.

THE REMARKABLE SWIFT PARROT
(LATHAMUS DISCOLOR)

Breeding and feeding

During spring and summer, swift parrots breed in natural hollows in Tasmanian blue gums (*Eucalyptus globulus*). The mother lays three to five eggs. She stays in the nest while the father searches for food.

Most parrots feed on seeds, but swift parrots mainly feed on nectar. Their favourite food when nesting is blue-gum blossoms. They scoop out the nectar with their brush-like tongues. They also eat the sugary lerps that insects deposit on gum leaves.

Swift parrots are messy eaters, but this makes them good **pollinators**. They spread pollen from tree to tree and make more flowers grow.

Researchers use **drones** and sightings by **citizen scientists** to identify swift parrot sites that need protecting. This is important work, as the swift parrot is now **critically endangered**. Only 750 of these beautiful birds may be left in the wild!

Migrating

Swift parrots are one of only two species of parrot that breed in Tasmania and **migrate** to the mainland every year. Before they

NORTHERN
TERRITORY

QUEENSLAND

WESTERN
AUSTRALIA

SOUTH
AUSTRALIA

NEW SOUTH
WALES

AUSTRALIAN
CAPITAL TERRITORY

VICTORIA

Winter range

BASS STRAIT

TASMANIA

Breeding range

leave their breeding sites in March, they fatten up on nectar so they can survive the 250-kilometre, nonstop flight across Bass Strait.

During autumn and winter, the parrots fly north through Victoria, the Australian Capital Territory, New South Wales and south-eastern Queensland, following the blossom trail in search of food. Researchers think that swift parrots travel up to 4000 kilometres each year – farther than any other parrot in the world!

Surviving

On mainland Tasmania, sugar gliders (*Petaurus breviceps*) threaten the survival of the swift parrot. These tiny possums were introduced into Tasmania around 150 years ago. They are small enough to clamber inside swift parrot nests, where they eat the eggs, the **hatchlings** and even the adult birds.

Scientists have invented nesting boxes with doors that shut automatically at night to keep sugar gliders out. But the swift parrots prefer their natural nesting hollows in Tasmanian blue gums. Luckily, sugar gliders do not live on some of the small islands off the coast of Tasmania, including Bruny Island near Hobart. There, the swift parrots can safely breed.

During their annual migration, swift parrots face many dangers. High winds blow them off course or out to sea. Domestic cats, feral animals and aggressive birds attack them. And because swift parrots fly at around 80 kilometres per hour – which makes them one of the fastest parrots in the world – they sometimes collide with mesh fences, cars and plate-glass windows.

The main threat to swift parrots is the loss of their **habitat** through logging, bushfires and land clearing for farming and urban development. To ensure swift parrots don't become **extinct**, we must protect their nesting sites in Tasmania and the eucalyptus trees they feed on in mainland Australia.

Helping swift parrots

Are there swift parrots in *your* backyard?
This is what to look for.

Size: Around 24 centimetres from head to tail, similar to rosellas and lorikeets

Nests: Hollow branches in **old-growth forests** in Tasmania

Habitat: Forests, woodlands and some areas in towns and cities with lots of trees

Sound: A bell-like tinkling, a chattering chirp or a 'pip, pip, pip' as they fly off

Food: Mainly nectar from blue-gum blossoms and lerps on flowering eucalypts

To help scientists track swift parrots, you can go to www.birdlife.org.au to record when these birds visit your backyard. You can also help protect them by sticking **decals** on large windows, covering mesh fences with shade cloth and keeping pet cats inside.

If you find an injured bird, first remove all threats, such as your pets. Then gently wrap the bird in a towel and place it in a secure, well-ventilated box. Put the box in a dark, quiet place and contact your local wildlife rescue organisation. WIRES, RSPCA and BirdLife Australia all have useful information on their websites about how to help injured birds. Note that baby birds sometimes fall from trees but it's often best to leave them alone and let their parents help them.

Glossary

Blossom trail The migration route followed by swift parrots, based on the flowering of gum trees

Canopy The leafy top of a tree

Chirruping Short, high-pitched bird sounds

Citizen scientists People who help scientists by gathering information

Critically endangered Facing an extremely high risk of extinction

Crowns The tops of birds' heads

Decals Pictures or patterns that stick on glass windows

Drones Small, remote-controlled aircraft

Extinct No longer in existence

Fledglings Young birds with flight feathers

Habitat A natural environment in which creatures live, grow and thrive

Hatchlings Chicks that have recently come out of the egg

Hollow A natural nesting hole in an old or dead tree, formed by burrowing insects or rotting wood

Lerps Sweet, waxy lumps on eucalypt leaves that contain young insects, known as larvae

Migrate Move from one place to another to breed and feed

Nectar Sugary liquid produced by flowers

Old-growth forests Ancient, undisturbed forests that have not been logged

Pollinators Animals, including insects, birds or small mammals, that spread pollen from one plant to another

Sugar gliders Small, gliding possums that feed at night

Acknowledgements

Thank you to my scientific advisor, Dr Debbie Saunders, Chief Executive Officer of Wildlife Drones Pty Ltd and Conservation Ecologist at The Australian National University's Fenner School of Environment and Society. Debbie alerted me to the plight of the swift parrot and provided invaluable professional expertise during the creation of this book.